Shelter on the Go

Written by Samantha Montgomerie

Collins

Tents keep out rain. They keep us snug.

Once, tents were like houses.

Mammoth-skin tents

Mammoth-skin tents were strong.

Tusks kept the roof up and the tent tight.

Teepees

Teepees were animal-skin tents with long sticks.

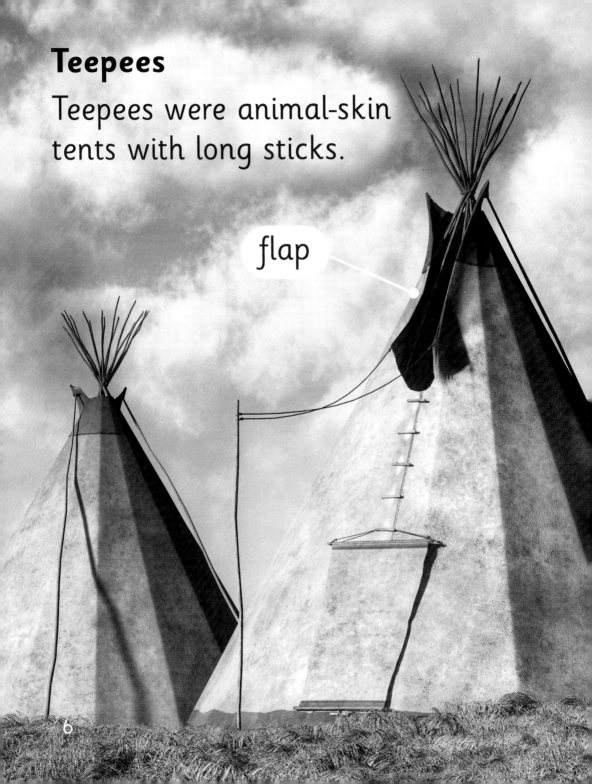

flap

Flaps let fresh air into the teepee.

7

Camps

When men went to fight, they had to set up a camp.

Tents were quick to pack up.

Shelter on the go

Herders travel with animals.

They camp in tents on long trips.

Modern tents

Now, tents are light.

cloth

They are quick to pack up. They are a tight fit in packs.

Shelter

15

After reading

Letters and Sounds: Phase 4

Word count: 98

Focus on adjacent consonants with short vowel phonemes, e.g. *strong*.

Common exception words: out, they, once, were, like, houses, the, into, when, to, go, are

Curriculum links: Understanding the world

Curriculum links (National Curriculum, Year 1): Design and technology; Geography

Early learning goals: Reading: read and understand simple sentences; use phonic knowledge to decode regular words and read them aloud accurately; read some common irregular words

National Curriculum learning objectives: Reading/word reading: read accurately by blending sounds in unfamiliar words containing GPCs that have been taught; Reading/comprehension: understand both the books they can already read accurately and fluently and those they listen to by checking that the text makes sense to them as they read, and correcting inaccurate reading

Developing fluency
- Your child may enjoy hearing you read the text.
- Ask your child to read the main text, making sure they notice the commas and full stops.

Phonic practice
- Practise reading words that contain adjacent consonants. Encourage your child to sound out and blend the following:

  snug   kept   fresh   trips   strong
- Can your child read these exception words? Which rhymes with far?

  were   the   are   out   like

Extending vocabulary
- Help your child make up a simple glossary for this book. Can they define:

  herders   camp   flap   mammoth   tusks